When Life Throws You a Curveball, Hit It

Simple Wisdom About Life's Ups and Downs

When Life Throws You a Curveball, Hit It

Simple Wisdom About Life's Ups and Downs

By Criswell Freeman, Psy. D.

WALNUT GROVE PRESS
NASHVILLE, TENNESSEE

WALNUT GROVE PRESS
P.O. Box 58128
Nashville TN 37205
(615) 320-9128

Library of Congress Catalog Card Number 94-66136

ISBN 0-9640955-0-5

Walnut Grove Press books are available at special discounts for bulk purchases for sales promotions, premiums, fund-raising, or educational use. For information contact Walnut Grove Press.

| *Book design* | Armour&Armour |
| *Cover design* | Mary Mazer |

Printed in the United States of America
by Horowitz/Rae Book Manufacturers, Inc.

2 3 4 5 6 7 8 9 10 ★ 95

To Mary Susan

and

To All My Business Associates
Who Courageously Took Their Swings

Contents

Introduction

Albert Einstein once said, "Make everything as simple as possible, but not simpler." With this in mind, I have written a book about the psychology of tough times. My interest in this topic springs from extensive studies in psychology *and* from personal experience.

By the time I was 35, I had achieved success as the world measures it. I headed a company that employed 1,500 people, housed 25,000 families, and was the fourteenth-largest residential landlord in America. I owned a piece of the American dream, complete with big house, company airplane, and mountain cabin.

In the late '80s, on the heels of a severely depressed real estate market, I experienced a financial setback that left me breathless. Eventually, I realized that I would have to start over from scratch. Such was my personal introduction to tough times.

After much thought, I decided to embark on a totally new career: psychology. I entered graduate school in Chicago and earned my doctorate, all the while gathering information for this text. In its original form, the book was longer and more technical in nature. It contained lots of psychological buzz words, impressive terminology, and plenty of advice.

But as I reread the manuscript, I remembered how I felt during my own hard times. I didn't have the energy to wade through technicalities, and I didn't want theories. I needed practical solutions, and I needed to hear them from someone who had been there.

This is the book I wish I could have read during my own tough times. I make no apologies for the uncomplicated nature of its message. Tough times cry out for solutions that are "as simple as possible, but not simpler."

Although these essays are straightforward, they are also "psychologically correct." The principles described in this book are espoused by mental health professionals from a variety of disciplines.

I am particularly indebted to Alfred Adler and his followers; to the cognitive-behavioral psychologists; to the Existential movement; and to Glasser's Reality Therapy. Casual readers may have little interest in the ways that these theories are woven into my stories, but they may be comforted to know that the ideas have been distilled from decades of study and research.

I am also indebted to my editor, Angela Beasley, who helped me condense the message into 18 brief essays.

This book was written out of my own experience. It combines the principles of modern-day psychology with the simple wisdom of common sense. If life has tossed you a curveball, don't despair. Simply keep reading, keep your spirits up, and above all, keep swinging.

When Life
Throws You
a Curveball,
Hit It

*"Courage is resistance to fear,
mastery of fear —
not absence of fear."*

Mark Twain
1835–1910

W HEN I WAS A KID, we played baseball in the Junior Knot Hole League. This was Nashville's version of the Little League, complete with uniforms, organized teams, and volunteer coaches. I can still recall the dusty fields, the sliding pads, and the uncomfortable spiked shoes,

Understand the impact of a curveball on a 10-year-old. This pitch bends as it approaches the plate, making it difficult to hit. Fastballs are tough enough, but curveballs? Forget it. Curveballs are murder.

Enter Ed White.

Ed White was the most feared pitcher in the Junior Knot Hole League, because he possessed a smoking fastball and a nasty curve. My teammates and I secretly dreaded the day when we would face the juggernaut White, but that day came and there I was, staring down the barrel of a loaded arm.

The first time I batted against Ed, I nearly jumped out of my cleats. His fastball had lots of zing, but it was the curve that made me want to turn in my uniform. Ed pitched and I flinched. My teammates and I spent the entire game dancing away from pitch after pitch; we couldn't hit the ball because our fears got in the way.

Only years later did I learn that a curveball is relatively easy to hit — under the right circumstances. A curve isn't as speedy as a fastball, and sometimes it doesn't break as much as the pitcher intends.

A batter with skill and patience can hit curveballs just as easily as other pitches, but he can't hit them if he's bailing out of the batter's box. He's got to stand in and face the pitch, like it or not.

Life is like Ed White. It is very good at throwing curveballs. While you're hoping for a straight pitch right over the plate, it's seldom that easy. Just when you think you have things figured out, the unexpected happens. Your life is proceeding just fine, and then — out of the blue — something goes wrong. Trouble arrives, ties your stomach in knots, and leaves you wondering if you'll ever get another hit.

Welcome to tough times.

Tough times come in all shapes and sizes: divorce, financial strain, job loss, and ill health, to name a few. When life takes a turn for the worse (as it does from time to time) you may be tempted to give up in disgust and turn in your uniform.

Not so fast. Maybe you don't need to quit — maybe you just need to learn a little more about hitting curveballs.

This book is about hitting life's curveballs. It's about overcoming your problems.
It is about facing reality and getting on with
your life. You can learn to control your emotions rather than allowing your emotions to
control you. And you can learn to hit life's
tough pitches if you're willing to practice
your batting.

You may be under the mistaken belief
that your problems are too complicated. You
may feel your situation is so unique and so
difficult that you'll never find a way out.
Thankfully, the lessons you'll need for overcoming tough times are simple ones — in fact
you've already learned them. You learned
them years ago as a child. This book is a
gentle reminder of those lessons.

What is the secret to hitting life's pitches?
To become a good curveball hitter, it takes
knowledge, courage, patience, and *practice.*
Your knowledge comes as you learn and live
through tough times. Talking with informed

people helps. So do books like this one. Whatever your problem, knowledge is power, so learn as much as you can.

You exhibit courage by standing at the plate and giving it your best effort, even when you are afraid. The more swings you take, the sooner your fears will subside. But don't expect to become a great curveball hitter overnight.

When tough times arrive, they usually overstay their welcome, so be patient. Expect gradual improvement as you continue to work on your problems, and your patience will be rewarded.

If you're having trouble hitting the pitches life has tossed your way, or if you know someone who is, read on. The first time you face that daunting curveball, you may flinch — you may even strike out. But with a little courage, a little knowledge, and a little practice, you can hit like a star. If that sounds appealing, turn the page.

And bring on Ed White.

Filling the
Tool Box

*"Man is a tool-using animal . . .
Without tools, he is nothing;
with tools, he is all."*

Thomas Carlyle
Scottish-born Author and Lecturer
1795–1881

BEFORE I RETURNED to graduate school to study psychology, I worked around apartment buildings. For 20 years, I leased and managed apartments, so I know a great maintenance man when I see one.

Alvin Wilson is a great maintenance man. Alvin loves his work and he's good at it, laboring with the care and confidence of a skilled craftsman. When he worked for my company, Alvin was the final word. That's why I often asked him to interview applicants for new maintenance positions.

Alvin had one overriding criterion, one absolute prerequisite for employment. At the end of each interview, he always asked the same question of all applicants.

He asked to see their tools.

This was the moment of truth. Many people can sound impressive in job interviews, but everyone doesn't possess a good set of tools. That's why Alvin never hired someone without first getting a close look at the person's tool kit. According to Alvin, tools spoke louder than words.

If the person owned no tools, that was a bad sign. If the tools were broken, lost, or in disarray, Alvin was not impressed. But, if an applicant produced a well-worn and well-stocked box of tools, it was time to start filling out payroll information.

Alvin's interviewing technique is more than a clever hiring strategy — it's a guide for better living.

If we wish to rise above life's inevitable challenges, we need tools. These tools aren't found in the local hardware store. They are the ideas, the relationships, and the behaviors that, if used regularly, mold us into better people.

You've probably been aware of these tools all your life. Parents, teachers, family, and friends have been endorsing them for years. The tool kit includes things like clear thinking, encouraging friends, sincere spirituality, and productive work. Proper rest, exercise, and diet are also important.

Tools allow us to face life with courage, helping us learn from our troubles and build better lives with the knowledge. The more we use the tools we've been given, the sooner we make repairs.

Some of the tools are familiar — others may have become a little rusty from disuse. You're invited to choose the ones that are right for you and place them in your kit. When you do, you'll be reacquainted with the following simple truths about tough times:

Working is better than waiting.

Fixing is better than blaming,

and . . .

The better your tools, the better your chances.

So when life tosses you a curve, remember Alvin. Be sure your tool kit is in order. Dust off the tools you were given as a child. You'll be surprised how well they still work, and you'll be amazed at the changes that will occur.

All because you decided to pull out that tool box and start filling it up.

Your Most Powerful Tool

*"A mind enlightened
is like heaven;
a mind in darkness is like hell."*

Chinese Proverb

TAKE A MOMENT to consider the miracle that is the human brain — the most complicated creation on earth. Composed of trillions of separate yet interconnected cells, your brain allows you to live, breathe, think, hope, and dream.

As you read these words, your heart continues to beat, your blood pressure and temperature are regulated, and a multitude of internal organs sustain your bodily functions.

Your eyes focus and refocus as you read down the page, and, without thinking, you hold the book in place. In addition, you have enough spare brainpower to think about the words you are reading. Amazing, isn't it?

Your brain never rests. Even while you sleep, it keeps working, never stopping for a single moment. It gives most of us a lifetime of service with very few mechanical problems. Though the brain contains trillions of moving parts, it's never closed for repairs — it just keeps doing the job, day after day.

Over a lifetime, your mind compiles a complicated, interwoven series of beliefs, hopes, wants, and needs. The result is your unique personality, one that is different from any other living human — past or present.

Considering it all, your brain is almost unbelievable in its miraculous powers. Possibly, you've been taking all this brainpower for granted. If so, it's time to reconsider. You have at your disposal the most powerful thinking apparatus ever created. That brain can become your best friend or your worst enemy, depending upon how you use it.

Given the brain's great potential, one thing seems clear:

Your mind is more powerful than your problems.

Use it as a problem-solving tool and watch it perform miracles. All that's required is clear thinking, realistic expectations, and a positive outlook.

But, just as your mind can be a wonderful tool for good, it can also become a self-imposed torture chamber. Tough times have a way of distorting your thoughts. Once your mind starts rolling down the highway of gloom, it quickly picks up speed. Soon, your problems seem hopeless because you've allowed the power of your mind to work against your best interests. This can make you miserable and cause physical harm. If that weren't enough, needless worry also inhibits your ability to think productively.

Ironically, the more you worry about your problems, the less likely you are to find solutions. You're simply too distraught to be effective. Instead of agonizing, convert that brainpower into productive thought. Here are some hints:

First, understand that most worries result from exaggerated thinking. As humans, we're programmed to make mountains of molehills. All of us do it from time to time. We possess the ability to imagine the worst and then worry about it.

Most of our fears never come to pass, but we worry about them as though they're already occurring. Silly behavior, but uniquely human.

You're probably telling yourself that things "must" turn out a certain way, that you "must" look good, or that you "must" get what you want. These messages are not realistic. If you're expecting life to always conform to your wishes, it's time for a healthy dose of flexibility coupled with a heaping helping of reality. Once you outgrow the illusion that life "must" unfold in a certain way, many of your worries simply fade.

If irrational fears arise, catch yourself in the act of worrying and interrupt the process before it gets out of hand. Take a few deep breaths. Quiet yourself, and regain the natural calm that will allow you to think more clearly.

In the beginning, you may find it helpful to write down the truth behind your fears. Examine the negative messages that you send yourself, and discover the exaggerations that hide behind them. Then have an honest talk with yourself and put things back into proper perspective.

Sometimes, you may find yourself upset over something of no consequence. For example, you may become terribly angered when someone cuts in front of you in traffic. Upon reflection, is someone else's poor driving enough reason to unleash the negative fury of your brain? Hardly. Instead of getting yourself all worked up, use rational, reality-based thinking. After a few minutes of self-talk, you'll feel better.

So when life throws you a curve, remember that you possess the greatest tool known to man: a human brain. It can be used constructively or not. Determine to make your brain a powerful problem-solving machine. After all, it's yours. So why not make it a useful servant rather than a cruel taskmaster?

Treat your brain as a "power tool" in the truest sense. Take care of it and use it wisely. If you do, there's no end to the things you can fix.

The Two Most Tiring Days

*"Real generosity toward
the future consists
in giving all
to what is present."*

Albert Camus
French Philosopher, Novelist,
and Dramatist
1913–1960

IF YOU'RE FACING tough times, you're probably tired. Tough times do that to you. They have a way of leaving you exhausted before the day has even begun. The weariness comes not from physical labor but from constant worry. That's why it's important to understand the source of your energy drain. Fatigue results from your attitude toward the two most tiring days: yesterday and tomorrow.

Why are yesterday and tomorrow so draining? They represent limitless reservoirs of exhaustion: the past and the future. If we could simply concern ourselves with the day at hand, life would be simple. But sometimes we lack both the ability to accept the past and the faith to accept the future.

As if today's tasks weren't enough, we take on the burdens of yesterday and the obligations of tomorrow. What a heavy workload! While fretting about the past, today's work goes wanting and tomorrow is put into jeopardy.

Interestingly, worry is a paradoxical phenomenon. For the most part, we worry about things that we are *not* doing. In fact, if we are deeply engrossed in an activity, it's impossible to agonize over it — we are simply too busy to be concerned.

Herein lies the paradox: Once we begin doing the thing that we're worried about, the worry subsides.

But if we ruminate about the past or fret about the future, we're inviting trouble. We turn the spotlight on ourselves, forgetting about the job that needs to be done. No wonder we're uneasy.

Here's a helpful remedy for anxiety. Become engrossed in the job at hand. Be willing to make a mistake, and be quick to forgive yourself when you do. With this attitude, you'll find anxiety evaporating into thin air. Concern yourself with today's work, and let the past and future fend for themselves.

What are yesterdays and tomorrows good for anyway? Yesterdays are custom-made learning tools. Stored away in our yesterdays are powerful lessons for improving our lives.

Tomorrows are for planning. By taking time to plan the future, we improve the chances of getting what we want from life, and that's good.

If you can learn from yesterday without undue regret, you are blessed. If you can plan for tomorrow without unproductive worry, you are wise. *Live your life in one-day packages*. Resolve to give this day your best effort, and find ways to enjoy it.

When you live in the present, there's little to worry about anyway. After all, the present is a very small sliver of time, suddenly upon us and too quickly gone. It's too precious to waste. So don't trouble yourself with those two terrible days, yesterday and tomorrow. And live the *only* day of the rest of your life … today.

Beyond Blame

"The fault, dear Brutus,
is not in our stars
But in ourselves. . . ."

From *Julius Caesar*
William Shakespeare
1564–1616

I N SEVENTH GRADE, I studied English under a teacher named Mrs. Bowen. She had a stern look that let you know she was all business. Her appearance was neat and proper. She was polite and respectful to students, but she could never be confused with a stand-up comedienne: no kidding around, no funny stories, no practical jokes. Just English and lots of it.

Margins had to be just so; spelling mistakes were harshly graded down; and punctuation had to be perfect. If you followed her rules and the rules of proper English, you had no problem. But woe to the poor student who turned in sloppy work. Mrs. Bowen showed no remorse as she flunked lazy students, and she expressed no trace of sadness as she handed back failing papers covered with red ink.

Mrs. Bowen and I didn't see eye-to-eye, and my grades showed it. I preferred to punctuate my own way; I spelled as the spirit moved me; and I completed assignments on my own timetable. Simply finishing my work would have been much easier than battling Mrs. Bowen, but I found concentrating on English impossible. As failing grades began to accumulate on my report card, I became more and more anxious. So instead of working harder, I did the natural thing.

I blamed Mrs. Bowen.

I told myself that her teaching skills were deficient. (They weren't.) I believed her expectations were unrealistic. (They weren't.) And I told any willing ear that she was terribly unfair. (She wasn't.) Because of my anger, I convinced myself that Mrs. Bowen was too hard, too strict, and too inflexible.

Finally, I decided that she simply didn't like me. In later years, I learned that Mrs. Bowen was actually quite fond of me — it was my work she didn't like.

Somehow, either by a miracle from God or by the mercy of Mrs. Bowen, I escaped her class with a final grade of "D." Not surprisingly, every English class after hers became a little easier. She taught English and she taught discipline, and I needed lessons in both. Today, I appreciate Mrs. Bowen, respect her, and remember her fondly.

But in seventh grade, I blamed Mrs. Bowen for my problems since she was the one handing out the failing grades. Obviously, the problem was mine, not hers, but I couldn't face my own shortcomings. So I spent time and energy blaming the instructor when I should have been studying the textbook. Such is the futility of blame.

When hard times arrive, it's easy to assign blame. We're quick to name culprits and anxious to curse them. Before we realize what's happened, we've worked ourselves into a grade-A frenzy. All for naught.

Unfortunately, the energy we invest in blaming others is wasted. The world offers no payoffs for those who collect injustices; the only reward is frustration.

Blaming others gives us fleeting satisfaction, so we usually keep a few scapegoats handy, just in case. We blame bosses, coworkers, parents, teachers, spouses, and even children. We may blame big government or big business. Once the blaming begins, anyone or anything is a potential target.

But blaming leads only to bitterness and ignorance; we become bitter because of imagined mistreatment, and we remain ignorant of our own shortcomings. Not surprisingly, we keep making the same old mistakes over and over.

Sometimes, we're innocent victims. But, more often than we'd like to admit, we've played some role in creating our tough times. There is actually great hope in this fact. It means that we have the power to make better grades whenever we get ready.

If life has been handing you some poor grades lately, concentrate on fixing things rather than affixing blame. It serves no good purpose to blame yourself for past mistakes — after all, you can't change yesterday. And there's no benefit in blaming others. Besides, they may be innocent.

Instead of looking for someone to blame, look for something to do. Instead of finding fault in others, look for the lessons that apply to you.

Instead of blaming the teacher, do the homework.

Because blame doesn't work. And as long as we're blaming, neither do we.

Waiting for Godot

*"While we are waiting,
life passes us by."*

Seneca
Roman Philosopher and Playwright
First Century A.D.

I N COLLEGE, I SAW a play called *Waiting for Godot*. It was required by a professor whose idea of a good time was a late-night poetry reading. The play wasn't just bad — it was torture. It was one of those plays that the critics love and the rest of us can't stand or understand.

The curtain went up, and the audience was treated to a couple of guys standing around on the stage, waiting for some fellow named Godot.

Who was Godot? They never really said. Why were they waiting? Your guess is as good as mine. When did they expect him to show? Any minute, except that Godot was always running a little late.

So I got to spend an entire evening watching a couple of actors argue, whine, complain, and — above all — wait. After two hours of non-stop moaning and groaning the play ended.

P.S. Godot never showed.

The next day in class, the professor informed us that the playwright, Samuel Beckett, won the Nobel Prize in '69. All I could say was that nobody asked for my vote.

Over the years, I've thought a lot about that crazy play, and I have a confession to make. I've mellowed. It's taken me 20 years to realize I'm glad that I went to see *Waiting for Godot*. I think I finally see what Beckett was trying to say.

The past 20 years have shown me that all of us do a little waiting for Godot. From time to time, all of us sit around and do nothing but complain. During these times, we secretly hope that someone will come along and solve our problems. Like the two fellows in the play, we sit and wait for somebody or something to bail us out.

But Godot doesn't show.

Oh sure, things may improve a little on their own, but real happiness remains elusive. No wonder. Godot probably has better things to do than solve our problems. For all we know, he may even have a few of his own.

Despite our good intentions, we sometimes lack motivation. When fear rules our thoughts, it's easy to procrastinate. We feel so discouraged that there seems to be no use in trying.

So we wait.

And wait. . .

and wait. . . .

The solution comes when we stop waiting and start working. After all, who says that anyone, even Godot, is going to go out of his way to solve our problems? And who says he could even if he wanted to?

Godot never showed once during the entire play — I'll bet he hasn't shown yet. And, if we wait around for tough times to get better on their own, we're really not much better than those two fellows in the play. We're in for a long wait, because when it comes to solving problems,

Working is better than waiting.

Waiting for things to improve is discouraging because control is out of your hands. But once you start to work, you realize that everything doesn't depend upon Godot or anyone else for that matter. It depends upon you.

Your happiness depends upon you. To a large degree, your health depends upon you. So does your financial well-being — the same goes for your relationships. The sooner you begin to work on these things, the sooner they begin to improve. The longer you wait around, the more things stay the same.

When you go to work, there's no time to become angry at Godot for his tardiness. You'll be so busy doing your job that it won't occur to you to blame poor Godot — Lord knows the two guys in the play have already done enough of that.

Do you have a problem that cries out for a solution? Are you discouraged, afraid, or anxious? Have you been postponing the inevitable? Have you been hesitant to act?

Get started anyway.

Despite your fears, go to work. Despite the anxiety, face your problem. Despite your discouragement, try anyway. When you do, you'll discover that working on solutions is better than dwelling on problems.

Once you go to work, you'll have the comfort of knowing you are intensely involved in your own solutions. And that's how it should be.

After all, who's got more at stake, you or Godot?

So don't wait for Godot to sweep in and fix everything. Just get busy, go to work, and see what happens. Even if the job seems overwhelming at first, get started. One small step is an important beginning.

I've decided if I ever have the free time, I'm going to write a play of my own — my response to Beckett. I'll call it *Stopped Waiting for Godot.* It will require no actors, and it certainly won't take two hours to perform. In fact, all that I'll need is a giant post-it note. The note will be about ten feet by ten feet and yellow. If I get a big budget, I might even have a huge refrigerator door to stick it on. As the curtain goes up, the audience will view a handwritten message on the note. It will read, "Dear Godot, I got tired of waiting. Decided to do it myself. Bye."

Who knows, I might even win a Nobel Prize.

The Bundle of Sticks

*"It is best to do things
systematically since
we are only human, and
disorder is our worst enemy."*

Hesiod
Greek Poet
Eighth Century B.C.

THE FIRST TIME I heard the story of the bundle of sticks, it was told to me by a Tennessee farmer. Then, I heard the same story from a bank president. Finally, an expert in Eastern philosophy told the same tale.

That makes it difficult to assign proper credit. I'm not sure whether it's a wonderful bit of backwoods lore, a metaphor for high finance, or a gem of wisdom from the Far East. I suppose it doesn't really matter, because anytime I hear something from so many different sources, there must be something to it. So here goes.

Imagine a thick bundle of sticks bound tightly together. Suppose someone asked you to break the bundle. If you attempted to break all the sticks at once, you'd be in trouble. In fact, it might be impossible. After hours of trying, what would you have to show for your efforts? Sore hands and a sour disposition.

Suppose, however, you tried a different tactic. Suppose you untied the bundle and proceeded to break each stick one at a time. You'd find this much easier.

Your problems are like that bundle of sticks. If you try to fix everything at once, you may fix nothing. Instead, you may undermine any chance of success, frustrating yourself in the process.

When we try to solve many problems at once, it's harder to solve *any* problems. We're too overwhelmed to be effective. Breaking the work into smaller packages makes impossible jobs possible.

Regrettably, we don't always tackle things one at a time. Most of us want our problems solved immediately, if not sooner! When troubles arrive in bunches, we want to fix them all — right now. Our impatience leads to wasted effort if we try in vain to break the unbreakable.

Sometimes it's difficult to untie the bundle of sticks. Our problems seem so interconnected that we can't see how to solve one without solving them all. We mistakenly tell ourselves that until everything is solved, nothing is solved, so we race from problem to problem, attempting "everything" and solving "nothing." The more we race, the more we worry, expending lots of energy but breaking no sticks.

With focus, solutions come easier. One solution leads to another. After the first stick breaks, we gain confidence. Soon, momentum is established and we're on our way.

Are you trying to break a bundle of sticks that's too thick to get your arms around? Pick out one problem and solve it.

One good solution is worth a thousand good intentions.

Instead of rushing from problem to problem, take time to organize your thoughts. Put pencil to paper if necessary. Once you've established your plan, go to work with all the gusto you can muster.

If you're distracted by other concerns, catch yourself in the act. Remind yourself that these are merely diversions. Focus on the single stick that lies before you, break it, and move onto the next. Soon, you'll have broken the entire bundle.

One stick at a time.

Chock-Full of Options

"Possibilities are infinite."

Thomas Fuller
English Writer and Cleric
1608–1661

UNLESS YOU'RE an astronomy buff, you probably don't pay much attention to the nighttime sky. You may notice the moon, a few big stars, or maybe a planet or two. And that's about it.

But if you want a treat, step outside on a dark, clear night and look up. If you're far enough from city lights, the spectacle will take your breath away. In addition to the obvious stars, you'll notice a fine white dusting of more distant ones. Each one of those tiny specks is a star the size of our sun — or larger. It's an impressive sight, but that's not half of it.

Point binoculars to the heavens and even more stars appear. Pause to consider that you're still viewing only a tiny fraction of our universe. In fact, you're not even seeing all the stars that make up our own Milky Way galaxy. And ours is only one of countless galaxies, each containing millions of stars.

The stars in the sky are literally too numerous to count. It's been estimated that there are more galaxies than there are stars in the Milky Way. Think of it. It's amazing to contemplate.

What does this little astronomy lesson have to do with tough times?

It's all about options.

When life tosses a curve, options seem to disappear like stars on a cloudy night. We look to the heavens but see only darkness. Our stars are there, but we can't see them because tough times obscure the view. Despite our limited vision, countless alternatives exist.

Often, we don't recognize options because of our own inflexibility. We want things to be a certain way, and we're unwilling to look at alternatives. As long as we keep the blinders on, we're stuck.

Until we consider our options, we have none.

When we allow ourselves to think creatively, choices become almost infinite. Once we open our eyes, options appear like bright stars on a crystal-clear night.

Are you feeling trapped by circumstances that seem unchangeable? They're not. Assess your alternatives. Even if you're stuck in an intractable situation, you can change the way you think, the way you feel, and the way you behave.

Like an astronomer searching for undiscovered stars, it's your job to search for new possibilities. Choices exist, even when you can't see them. Inflexibility has temporarily clouded your vision. Begin a creative search for solutions. Soon the clouds will part, and you'll be viewing a beautiful sky.

Chock-full of options.

A Presidential
Prescription for
Embarrassment

"Time is a great physician."

Benjamin Disraeli
English Statesman and Novelist
1804–1881

THE NIGHT PRESIDENT Nixon resigned, I was singing country music. During my brief musical career, I was never confused with Hank Williams, and our band never made it to the charts. In fact, our greatest brush with fame came during an extended summer engagement at the Holiday Inn in Stark, Florida.

Although this was not the nation's most glamorous venue, we weren't complaining. We were four college guys having a good time earning money doing something we loved.

In the summer of '74, President Nixon was in deep trouble over Watergate. Some very intelligent people had done outrageous things resulting in the first resignation of a United States president.

On that balmy August night, we carefully timed our first break to watch Nixon's historic announcement. When we got back to the room and turned on the television set, there he was, with a deathly pallor, sweating profusely, saying goodbye.

As the President resigned, I couldn't help feeling sorry for the man. Although Mr. Nixon was a bright and successful guy, he had committed a colossal blunder. Now he had to admit his mistakes and take his medicine in front of millions. Talk about embarrassing.

After Nixon finished his speech, my band members and I returned to the lounge to begin our second set. The place was still smoky; waitresses were still serving drinks; and the patrons were still sitting around doing the things that people do in bars. I announced that we had a new president, but few people seemed concerned. They weren't interested in long speeches or political analyses; they just wanted to hear country music. Someone in the crowd yelled, "Play *The Tennessee Waltz!*" and that was that. Back to twanging guitars and cold beer.

So much for history in the making.

That night I learned an important lesson about embarrassing moments: No matter how big the problem, life is bigger. Even the resignation of a president doesn't change things that much. For a while, there are headlines, editorials, and news bulletins. But soon, people go back to drinking beer and requesting *The Tennessee Waltz.*

Like Mr. Nixon, we find ourselves in embarrassing situations, and we hate to have our imperfections made public. After all, our society idealizes success and prosperity. Hard times may mean embarrassing circumstances (like job loss, bankruptcy, or divorce). In spite of the old adage about sticks and stones, it still hurts.

I've sometimes wondered how much Nixon would have minded quitting if nobody had known. After all, the job paid less than he could have made as a high-priced lobby-ist in a big Washington law firm. Plus, think of all the headaches that go along with being president. There's never a minute of peace. Nonetheless, as president of the United States, he couldn't quit without a lot of people know-ing, so he was stuck.

Some of us, like Nixon, are stuck doing things that we don't enjoy, but we're too em-barrassed to quit. So we work in frustration for years, waiting for improvements that never come. This speaks volumes about the power of peer pressure. In truth, many of us are controlled not by our own wishes but by the fear of what others might think.

If you're feeling tyrannized by the opin-ions of others, remember that nobody cares as much as you think they do. No matter how big a problem may seem to you, it's probably not very big to the rest of the world. It's easy to imagine that you're at the center of everyone's thoughts. You're not. Your mountain is your neighbor's mole hill.

It's not that people are insensitive. It's just that, when it comes to troubles, they have their own — yours naturally take second billing. Even a president's problems don't hold people's attention for long.

So lighten up. Don't allow embarrassment to turn you into a hermit. Learn to laugh at yourself. If you're feeling embarrassed about past mistakes, stop! Get over the embarrassment and start laughing again.

One evening, almost two decades after Watergate, I was clicking through the channels and there he was. Nixon — the man who experienced so much pain on that hot night in August of '74. Looking calm, wise, and self-assured, he was talking about global affairs and making a lot of sense.

Whether you like him or not, you've got to admire the way that he came back from his problems. He wrote several books and became a sought-after expert on foreign affairs — all after his resignation. Plus, he wasn't afraid to go on television and let big-shot newscasters ask him lots of questions. Now that's guts.

Despite the long odds, Nixon made a comeback.

I'm sure some people remember Nixon as the fellow who got us out of Vietnam and opened up trade with China. Good work to be sure. They may occasionally ponder his tough times back in '74. But not me — when I think of Mr. Nixon, something else comes to mind . . . *The Tennessee Waltz.*

Taking Care of
the Equipment

*"There are no riches above
a sound body."*

Ecclesiastes 30:16

I N THE SAME YEAR that Nixon resigned, a book came out called *Zen and the Art of Motorcycle Maintenance.* It was another one of those literary masterpieces that everybody seemed to understand but me. Critics raved. Intellectuals debated. Libraries ordered extra copies. And I scratched my head.

The motorcycle maintenance I could understand, but the Zen wasn't getting through. I gave the book my best shot, but after about 100 pages, I called it quits. Too much digging for not enough gold.

Fast forward 20 years. In a bookstore, I happened to see that familiar purple cover. It was the same book, only this time in its thirty-fifth printing. Thirty-fifth printing? Surely, I told myself, there must be a message in there somewhere. So in the name of curiosity, I bought a copy, went home, and started digging again.

This time, I found the gold. Twenty years later, the author finally made sense. His was the story of a cross-country motorcycle trip, but it was much more than a travelogue. The author, Robert Pirsig, described the great satisfaction of maintaining a motorcycle in tip-top condition. He loved his motorcycle and did most of the work on it himself.

Pirsig marveled at the bike, admiring its beauty and symmetry. He carefully studied each engine part. He reveled in the craft of motorcycle maintenance in a way that was, somehow, inspirational. He described the details of changing spark plugs, draining oil, and tuning the engine. For Pirsig, this was a religious experience. No doubt about it — that fellow was crazy about motorcycles. Especially his own.

What, you have every right to ask, do motorcycles have to do with a book about tough times? The answer concerns maintenance. When tough times hit, you need to care for your physical health in the same way that Pirsig cared for his bike. You deserve the same meticulous treatment.

Tough times are hard on the equipment. We're so worried about our problems that physical health takes a back seat. We're too tired to exercise. A decent night's sleep is something we only dream about. Proper diet goes the way of the tropical rain forest.

To make matters worse, we tend to "reward" ourselves with unhealthy goodies like ice cream, Twinkies, six-packs, and chips. These rewards pay short-term dividends but may exact a painful price in the long run.

Your first job during tough times is maintaining your strength — physically, emotionally, and spiritually. As long as you maintain your health, other problems assume secondary importance.

Possibly, you've experienced frustration in the past and may have reservations about your ability to stick to a healthy lifestyle. Maybe you've been on a few diets that didn't work. (Who hasn't?) Possibly you've made some New Year's resolutions that you didn't keep. (Welcome to the club.) Don't let past indiscretions get you down. Simply start a physical-fitness program with a new attitude.

Typically, people concentrate on things they must give up like sweets, booze, and so on. For a change, concern yourself only with things that you'll be getting: the rewards of better health.

Start a physical-fitness program slowly. If you're just beginning to exercise, consult a physician. Be careful and consistent. In a short time, you'll begin to see changes that will surprise and gratify you.

See yourself as your body's master mechanic. As you begin to treat your body with proper respect, you'll feel better and you'll walk with your head held a little higher.

Soon, you'll see old indulgences for what they really are: threats to your happiness and to your life. You'll become more concerned with the only physical equipment that you'll possess in this lifetime: your body. Like Robert Pirsig, you'll be the proud owner of a machine that you understand and respect.

Which brings me back to the reason I didn't understand Pirsig's book when it first came out in 1974. I was only 20 years old at the time. Young people seem to take their bodies for granted, assuming that good health is a permanent birthright. I was no different. Good maintenance? Peace of mind? Who needed it? Maybe I thought I would last forever.

Twenty years later, I know better.

The Magic of
Encouragement

*"A friend is a present
you give yourself."*

R.L. Stevenson
Scottish Poet, Novelist, and Essayist
1850–1894

GROWING UP, I WAS a San Francisco Giants fan. In those days, a guy's favorite player was either Willie Mays or Mickey Mantle. I liked Mays, so the Giants were my favorite team. That's why I've always been a little sad that I wasn't old enough to witness the most wonderful moment in Giants' history.

It was '51 and the team was still playing in New York; Truman was president; and Willie Mays was a fresh-faced rookie. The National League season ended in a tie for first place: A playoff was required to determine the champion.

It was the bottom of the ninth in the final game with the Giants trailing the arch-rival Brooklyn Dodgers by a score of 4-2. The championship was on the line, and across the country fans sat spellbound by their radios as Bobby Thomson came to the plate. With runners on second and third, Dodgers' pitcher Ralph Branca knew all too well that Thomson represented the winning run.

On Branca's second pitch, Thomson connected. Everyone in the park heard that familiar crack as they saw the ball leap from the bat. Back. Way back! Home run!

"The Giants win the pennant! The Giants win the pennant! The Giants win the pennant...."

Bobby Thomson circled the bases and was mobbed at home plate by fans and teammates in one of the singular moments of baseball history. Oh, to have been a Giants fan on that day back in '51. Think of the satisfaction. Imagine the excitement, the thrill, the joy.

But imagine how Ralph Branca must have felt.

From time to time, all of us feel the kind of pain that Branca must have felt that day. We make a mistake and it costs us. Maybe it's not so public as Ralph Branca's fateful pitch, but it hurts just as much.

This is a world that glorifies winners. When we hit the game-winning home run, there are sure to be people standing at home plate ready and waiting to share the triumph.

Tough times are different — they're harder to share. We would prefer to close ourselves off from others, but that's when we need other people most.

Many of us wait for encouragement to find us. In reality, it's our job to find it. If we find the right kind of support, tough times are easier to handle. But, if we leave matters to chance, we may find ourselves fighting a losing battle.

Encouragement, like friendship, must be earned. You earn it by opening yourself up to family and friends.

Sometimes, encouraging friends simply show up on the doorstep, willing to help. It's your job to invite them in. Other times, it seems as though you haven't a friend in the world. On those occasions, it's up to you to go out and prove yourself wrong.

Encouragement can be a ticket out of tough times, but beware: There are two kinds of encouragement, real and imitation. Real encouragement leaves you believing that you possess the strength to solve your own problems. It lifts you up, making self-pity impossible. Encouraging friends may suffer with you, but they will never pity you. Instead, they'll remind you of your strengths and resources.

After talking with an encouraging friend, you will feel invigorated. You'll possess a faith that will soon translate into action. Your faith is not foolish optimism nor is it self-delusion. It's a realistic assessment of your abilities.

But all encouragement is not created equal. Sometimes, encouragement is actually discouragement in disguise. On the surface, the words you hear seem helpful, but, in truth, they leave you less sure of yourself than before you heard them. Sometimes, this discouragement masks itself as pity. Other times, the message concerns the misfortune of another poor soul whose trouble is greater than your own. Neither message is helpful.

Friends who pity you usually mean well, but they do harm. They leave you with feelings of weakness and dread. Their message is usually a reflection of their own insecurities. *They* feel uneasy and, before long, so do you. Such conversations leave you disheartened about the future. The unspoken message is that you're unlucky, mistreated, and helpless. This is false advertising and contrary to your best interests.

The best way to distinguish between encouraging and discouraging messages is to examine your own feelings. After you spend time with discouraging friends, you see little hope for the future. Your stomach is tied in knots, and you have no plan of action. Encouraging friends are different. They help you formulate specific plans for the future. They don't waste time recounting the misfortunes of others. Their suggestions leave you energized and hopeful.

Some of the most discouraging people in the world are genuinely well-meaning. They don't intend to make you abandon hope, but they do so with remarkable skill. To avoid feeling gloomy and not knowing why, avoid the gossips, the pessimists, and the self-righteous. Don't listen to the whiners who think things are hopelessly unfair. And ignore the nay-sayers who believe that mistakes are impossible to repair.

Distinguish between discouraging and encouraging friends, and start spending time with the right crowd.

After all, who really needed an encouraging friend on that day back in '51, Bobby Thomson or Ralph Branca?

Too Many
Coat Hangers

*"The cost of a thing
is the amount of life
which is required to be
exchanged for it."*

Henry David Thoreau
American Essayist and Novelist
1817–1862

COAT HANGERS are wonderful. Imagine your closet without them. Coat hangers don't cost much; they're universally available; and, they almost never wear out. How many products can claim that?

Yes, coat hangers are terrific — until you have more than you need. Then they become a pain in the closet.

When it comes to coat hangers, more isn't necessarily better. Let your closet become overloaded with unused hangers, and you've created a haberdasher's nightmare. Extra hangers become tangled up in everything. They take up space, obscure clothes, and generally make a mess of things. Before you know it, you're spending more time unraveling hangers than you are selecting your wardrobe.

Most things in life are like coat hangers. There's a right amount, and then there's too much. Find the right amount, and life becomes a little easier. Become overloaded, and you're in trouble.

We live in a society that assumes more is better. No wonder. Every day we are bombarded with advertising that tempts us to buy newer, more expensive gadgets to replace the older, less expensive ones we bought last year. Beautiful, young models sell us everything from soap suds to six-packs. The messages are subtle but powerful: Buy what they're selling and enjoy the good life. Even though we know better, we fall for it time and again.

Our mistaken desire for "more" can bring on tough times. Sometimes, we cause our own misery by overbuying or over-committing. When we do, we create a tangled web of problems that resembles a closet overloaded with hangers. And there's only one thing to do.

Simplify.

Simplicity has much to recommend it and would be a terrific product to sell except for one fact — nobody can earn a profit promoting it. You won't hear a celebrity making a paid endorsement for simplicity. And you'll never gaze into the eyes of a gorgeous model who asks you to slow down, stop spending, and pare down your lifestyle.

Fortunately, there have been many wise men and women who did champion the simple life: Henry David Thoreau, Mother Teresa, and the man from Galilee to name a few. But their voices are too often drowned out by the din of commercialism. Consequently, we live in a world where simplicity is hard to find and even harder to keep.

That's why it's important to be able to say "No." Until you can say "no" to things you don't need, you're asking for trouble.

Have you gone through a life-changing experience that has left you with a clean slate? Look upon it as an opportunity.

Have you lost some material possessions that you really didn't need? Say a word of thanks.

Are you working 60 hours a week in order to pay for things that you don't have time to enjoy? Live with less and enjoy yourself more.

Once you begin to simplify, you'll wonder why you ever wanted it any other way. You'll also learn an important lesson about life: Too many hangers don't ensure a happy closet.

They prevent it.

Taking Control

"We are our choices."

Jean-Paul Sartre
French Philosopher, Writer, and Critic
1905–1980

I LIVE IN NASHVILLE and have a few friends in the music business. A couple of them knew Elvis.

Every time I run into somebody who had any personal contact with The King, I ask the obvious: "What happened?" How did a guy who had everything meet such a tragic end? Usually, I get the same answer.

Elvis lost control.

He lost control of his business affairs. He lost control of his appetite. He lost control of his career. Gradually, he surrounded himself with people who encouraged these excesses. Hangers-on granted Elvis's every wish, fearing anyone who said "no" would be fired.

No one was able to control Elvis, and

soon he was unable to control himself. So there he was, the great Elvis Presley, a man with everything — everything except control of his own life.

Without control, Elvis was an accident waiting to happen. And it happened.

You and I are not very different from Elvis. When we lose control, bad things start happening. When we fall prey to bad habits and sloppy thinking, troubles begin to accumulate like overdue bills. Eventually, it's time to pay up.

When we lose control, logical thinking goes out the window. What results is self-inflicted propaganda of major proportions.

Sometimes, we tell ourselves "All is well" when it's not. By denying the need for change, we allow little troubles to mushroom into big ones.

Other times, we become overly pessimistic. We tell ourselves "All is lost, there's no hope, and nothing can be done." We take these thoughts at face value, assuming that because we think them, they must be true.

Usually, they aren't.

Most of our worries are inflated, bearing scant resemblance to reality. Yet, we accept them as though they were handed down by God Himself.

The truth is much less sinister: All is not lost (unless we convince ourselves that it is); there is hope (unless we stop hoping); and, there is much productive work to be done (unless we choose to ignore it).

Worry isn't something that we have; it's something that we do.

Where do worries go when we're not worrying? Nowhere. They don't exist until we start them up. You and I don't have worries until we start worrying. Likewise, you and I don't have control until we seize it.

Sometimes, we live under the illusion

that we have little or no control over our attitudes and moods. Thankfully, this is untrue. To a great extent, we create our attitudes and moods when we select the things we think about.

While one person stops to admire a rose bush, another sees nothing but thorns. One person is uplifted while the other is embittered: same bush, different perspectives.

If you find yourself thinking gloom and doom, think again. Take control of your thoughts. Talk to trusted, encouraging friends. Begin keeping a journal. Take a few minutes of quiet time each day in order to keep your priorities straight. Take more time to think productively and less time to worry.

Carefully note the important difference between the things that you can control and the things that you can't. Work diligently on the former and forget about the latter. That's the essence of wisdom. And it's the epitome of control.

Speaking of control, what if Elvis had possessed more control over his thoughts and
behaviors? I'm confident that things would
have been different. At some point, he would
have gotten the wake-up call. He would have
fired all the hangers-on, dumped the drugs
down the garbage disposal, and cleaned up
his life.

If Elvis hadn't lost control, he might still
be alive today, looking good and making the
world a happier place. His name could still
be up in lights, and he could still be a living,
breathing inspiration to millions.

Sadly, it's too late for Elvis to assume control over his thoughts and actions.

But what about the rest of us?

The Dropped Pass

*"My life has been nothing
but a failure."*

Claude Monet
French Impressionist Painter
1840–1926

HAVE YOU EVER made a mistake in front of a lot of people? Unless you're a hermit, you probably have. If so, you know the sinking feeling that accompanies public failure. And you'll understand how I felt on a terrible day back in 1963.

It was November 22, the same day that President Kennedy was assassinated. I was a nine-year-old boy playing elementary school football. That afternoon, our team met a nearby rival in a game that, to me, seemed historic.

The other team's biggest weapon was a speedster named Jimmy Elrod. Elrod was little, fast, and tough — a touchdown threat any time he handled the ball. Our star was quarterback Big Mike Regan. It was no surprise when we scored first with a long bomb — Regan to me. Seven zip.

Elrod answered with two quick touchdowns of his own. After missing both extra points, they still led 12 to 7. That's the way it stayed until late in the game.

With little time on the clock, we were closing in on a touchdown when Mike called my number. If I made the catch, we'd win the game. Regan yelled "Hike!" and I took off into an open area safely behind enemy lines. Thirty years has passed, but I can still see the perfect spiral on the ball as it left Mike's hand in apparent slow motion. I can still hear the hush of the crowd, and I can still feel the texture of the pigskin as it lightly touched my fingertips.

And I can still sense my stunned horror as the ball brushed past my fingers and fell to the ground. Incomplete pass.

A few plays later the game ended and we lost. Elrod and his teammates acted like they'd won the Super Bowl. They yelled and hugged for what seemed like an eternity. That only made my pain more intense.

I felt like a total failure.

As an adult, it's easy to put fourth-grade athletics into perspective. These games are not nearly as important as they seem to nine-year-old boys. In truth, I was never a "failure" for dropping the ball. I was simply a little boy trying hard — maybe too hard.

When a child labels himself a failure, we are quick to correct him, and rightfully so. But when grown-ups make mistakes, the labeling sticks. We adults take winning and losing very seriously. If we face loss in business, marriage, or finance, we feel like total failures — we may even brand ourselves as such.

We beat ourselves up. We see ourselves as "bad." We pigeonhole ourselves and then live with self-sabotaging guilt that is undeserved. By labeling ourselves, we create negative attitudes that are difficult to exorcise.

When I think back to that '63 football season, I realize that no other person on earth remembers that game like I do. A few people may have some hazy recollections, but no one has a vivid memory of my dropped pass. That pass was important to me and nobody else. Was I a failure? Only in my own mind.

Have you dropped a pass in the game of life? Are you still beating yourself up for some past mistake? Stop the name-calling. Forgive everybody, including yourself.

Then get on with the game. After all, you still have lots of passes to catch.

Sad About Cris

*"Sadness flies on the
wings of morning,
and out of darkness
comes the light."*

Jean Giraudoux
French Dramatist, Novelist, and Diplomat
1882–1944

WHEN CRIS DIED, he was nine and I was seven.

Cris was my dog, a feisty little black-and-white mutt, one of those dogs that everybody loved instantly. To seven-year-old boys, dogs are a lot like people, and Cris was no exception. He was more like a brother than a pet. So it was no surprise that the news hit hard when they called to say that he had been hit by a car and killed.

That night, when I returned home from my grandmother's, I wasn't the only one cry-ing. The whole family was overcome. My parents had adopted Cris from the pound two years before their first baby arrived. He was a full-fledged member of the family, and the loss was a terrible blow.

A kind neighbor had already taken the body to the local animal shelter, so I never saw Cris again. Ever. But my father did a very wise thing that made the pain a little easier to take.

He had a funeral.

It wasn't exactly a funeral because there was nothing to bury — the earthly remains were long since gone. But we had a funeral anyway. The family got together, held hands, cried, talked about Cris, and said a prayer. That funeral somehow made the loss easier to accept.

Funerals serve a purpose. They give us time to feel our loss and express our sadness. By doing so, we move through the process of grieving, ultimately moving forward with our lives. When people die, we're accustomed to funerals. But when it comes to other losses, we sometimes forget to bury the dead.

Thirty years after Cris died, I faced a different kind of loss: the loss of my business. Ours had been a family-owned real estate concern founded by my grandfather long before I was born. Economic forces drove me into a merger with a local competitor — to me, this was the same as a loss. I was left to close up shop.

What a terrible time in my life. . . . I suffered sleepless nights, crushing stress, and untold guilt. As business activities wound to a close, I was preoccupied with bankers, lawyers, employees, and reporters. A funeral was the furthest thing from my mind.

Several years passed. Eventually, I left the field of real estate altogether, moving to Chicago in pursuit of a doctorate in psychology. Still, the loss of my business haunted me at every turn. One day, I was sitting in a class-room listening to a lecture on grief, and it hit me.

It was time for another funeral.

Upon my return to Nashville, I headed straight for my old office building — by now, any trace of my business was gone. A carpet company had moved into the ground floor. Lawyers' offices occupied some of the build-ing. An engineering firm had taken up resi-dence in space once used by our accounting department. Things were certainly different now, but that wasn't important.

I stood in the parking lot, looking at sur-roundings that had once been so familiar.

And I had a private service.

Is there something in your life that needs to be buried? If so, bury it. Grieve it, cry about it, even have a funeral if necessary. Whether it's a lost job, a broken relationship, or a shattered dream, it needs to be mourned.

We live in a society that doesn't take much time to heal its wounds. When we lose things of great importance, we're often encouraged to go about our business as though nothing happened. And we don't take time to feel the pain.

A better strategy is to accept the loss, grieve for a while, and then get on with living. If you've lost something important, don't be embarrassed to have a funeral. If you feel comfortable, invite family and friends. If not, do it by yourself. Even if the loss is a very old one, pay your respects.

Because funerals serve a purpose.

It's never too late to have a private service.

Faith in the Lost and Found

*"Begin to weave and
God will give the thread."*

German Proverb

I N KINDERGARTEN we had a lost and found box. It was simple cardboard adorned with colored construction paper. Whenever something of value was misplaced, the teacher pointed to that little box and, sure enough, the lost item was usually there.

Did you lose a mitten? Look in the lost and found. Missing the scarf your mother knitted? Ditto. Lost that fat pencil or your favorite pair of scissors? Go check the lost and found.

The lost and found never contained great material riches. If you were searching for bundles of cash, you had to look elsewhere. But if you wanted to retrieve something personal — something that was uniquely yours — the lost and found was the place to go.

In life, as in kindergarten, it's easy to lose things. But grown-up losses can be much more painful than disappearing scarves or unclaimed mittens. Grown-ups can lose wealth, prestige, even health. These hurts are troublesome . . . sometimes devastating. But the greatest loss of all has nothing to do with earthly possessions. It has to do with faith.

When life tosses a curveball, it's easy to lose faith.

We lose faith in ourselves.

We lose faith in the future.

We lose faith in other people.

We may even lose faith in God.

Amidst the confusion, we may stray from sources of spiritual strength. It's not that we do so intentionally. It's just that we're faced with so many unanswered questions. We can't seem to find time for something as esoteric as faith. After all, there are things to be done, bills to be paid, and worries to be worried.

As hope slips through the cracks, a new belief system replaces the old. We believe the worst. We lose confidence in the future; we see no meaning for our lives; and, we sink into the despair of depression.

Depression is negative faith. It is the expectation of a future without joy. It is belief in a world without hope. It is the conviction that life can not be repaired.

Sometimes depression results from physical causes — the obvious cure is medicine. But many times, sadness stems from a spiritual crisis.

If you've encountered a life-changing challenge, faith may be in short supply. It's possible that you're asking yourself the wrong questions. You may be asking "Why me?"

when you should be asking "What now?"

When you ask "Why me?" you concentrate on the unfairness of your personal situation. You may blame yourself, other people, or even God. As long as you remain stuck in the "Why me?" mode, you're focused on past disappointments.

When you ask "What now?" you focus on the things you *can* do. You use your experience to help others. You discover new meaning for your life — meaning that incorporates all your experiences, good and bad.

The sooner you can move from "Why me?" to "What now?" the sooner you'll be on the road out of tough times. And the sooner you'll experience spiritual renewal. Your spiritual renewal is a personal matter. It may include quiet introspection, prayer, or worship. You may find renewal in the silent beauty of a sunrise or the blooming of a flower. Wherever you find your strength, go there often.

When life takes a turn for the worse, peek into your spiritual lost and found. Know that your faith has not been destroyed; it's just been hidden from view. Once you decide to search for it, you won't have to look very far.

Spiritual health is a powerful gift you give yourself. When you're ready to ask the right questions, spiritual treasures await. Those treasures are yours — and they're safely tucked away nearby. Why not claim them right now?

Perspective in
a Cemetery

*"The present will not
long endure."*

Pindar
Greek Poet
Fourth Century B.C.

W HEN LIFE HANDS US unexpected troubles, it's easy to allow small problems to assume enormous proportions. When we're overwhelmed, inspiration and wisdom are elusive, but there's a place where we can find both:

The cemetery.

I know what you're thinking. What self-respecting self-help author would recommend a visit to the graveyard? Me, for one.

And what, you ask, could possibly be uplifting about a cemetery? Just this. In fewer days than we might imagine, this earthly journey will be over. The sadness will be gone and the wounds will be healed.

No earthly problems are permanent, and that's good news. By remembering this fact, we observe the ironclad rule for overcoming tough times — we keep things in perspective.

Sometimes, perspective is hard to come by. We have difficulty distinguishing between big problems and little ones. Often, we fail to realize an important truth: Most of our problems are little problems.

Without perspective, we take little troubles and blow them into big ones. Money becomes a big problem. Work becomes a big problem. The opinions of others assume great importance. We take any of a thousand nuisances and convince ourselves that they are big, important problems. But they're not.

Big problems concern health. Unless your problem concerns spiritual, physical, or psychological health, it probably isn't as big as you think. As long as you and your loved ones possess the gift of health, consider yourself lucky. And, consider your problems small ones.

Worrying too much about little problems guarantees big ones. Unless we're careful, we gradually allow little problems to balloon into big trouble. We can become sick, depressed, or anxious.

We worry about a bigger house, a newer car, or a quicker promotion. We worry about things that our neighbors are saying. We worry about things we can't control and things we cannot change. We worry about savings accounts, income taxes, and mortgage balances — little problems all.

For many of us, perspective comes only after hardship or loss. Until our spirits are shaken to their very foundation, we find ourselves dwelling on minor inconveniences while ignoring life's greatest joys. Instead of treasuring life, we take it for granted. We miss a beautiful sunset because we're watching the evening news.

We live as though we would live forever, fully knowing we won't. That's why it's helpful to find perspective in a cemetery.

Standing near the graves of those who have gone before, we receive a healthy dose of reality. If we're attentive, voices from beyond the tombstones have much to tell us. They instruct us to look at the rose instead of the thorn. They ask us to think less of ourselves and more of others. They challenge us to walk through the world with our eyes and our hearts open.

The next time you're faced with tough times, ask yourself if this is a problem that will concern you on your death-bed. If not, don't disturb yourself too much.

Size up problems before they ruin your life. Separate little ones from big ones, imagined ones from real ones, and controllable ones from uncontrollable ones. Accept the ones you can't change without exaggerating the rest, and go to work. You may be surprised. Most troubles are not as big as they first appear.

Have you got big problems? Take them to the cemetery. Have a quiet chat with the people who are resting there. See if they can help you put things into perspective.

Changing the End
of the Story

"Nothing endures but change."

Heraclitus
Greek Philosopher
Fifth Century B.C.

I'VE HEARD IT SAID that Howard Hughes used to watch an old movie called *Ice Station Zebra*. I don't know much about the film, but I think it starred Ernest Borgnine and was a story about an outpost at the North Pole. It was rumored that Hughes watched the movie hundreds, possibly thousands, of times.

It's not the fact that Mr. Hughes supposedly watched films almost every night. Millions of people do that. It's the fact that he watched *the same* film night after night. Now that's unusual.

155

Watching *Ice Station Zebra* a thousand times seems crazy since the movie never changes. I'm as big an Ernest Borgnine fan as the next guy, but nobody's good enough to watch every night. After all, reruns never change.

Thankfully, our lives are not like movies. We have the power to change our stories any time we get ready. We don't have to watch the same scenes a thousand times; instead, we can transform our stories while we live them.

During hard times, our stories become troubling, but it doesn't have to end there. Until the curtain closes, the conclusion remains unwritten, and there's always time to rewrite the script.

You're the writer, producer, and star of your own story, so why not take control?

Forget about blaming others. Simply rewrite your part and start the cameras rolling. . . .

If you don't like the scenery . . .
switch sets.

If you don't like your role . . .
become a new character.

If your cast gets you down . . .
audition new players.

If your story screams for action . . .
direct it.

Encouraging friends will help shoulder the load. And you'll do your part by maintaining perspective while working diligently on your problems. You'll avoid the traps of blame and envy. You'll overcome the unfounded worries that, in the past, led to hesitation and doubt. And you'll proceed without undue fear of failure.

Slowly at first, and then more quickly, you'll see changes. You won't repeat the same old mistakes. Instead, you'll craft a new, improved story — one that brings you pleasure and fulfillment.

So don't believe for a minute that you're trapped in a script you can't change. Your life story isn't complete. Certainly, like all of us, your story contains ups and downs. It holds successes and failures, wins and losses, joys and heartbreaks. But your story is far from over. Like any suspenseful script, we can't be certain how things will end until we turn the final page.

That ending is up to you.

May yours have a joyous and triumphant conclusion.

Epilogue

Has life thrown you a curveball?

Have you experienced hardship and survived?

Unless you're very young or very lucky, you've faced a few curveballs. The world occasionally hands out unwelcome surprises to all of us. It's not pleasant, but it's life.

Maybe you became a better person because of your close encounter with tough times. Or maybe you discovered a creative solution to a very tricky problem.

If you have an interesting, inspirational, or funny story, I'd like to hear it. Please write me with your own curveball story at the following address:

> Criswell Freeman
> c/o Walnut Grove Press
> P.O. Box 58128
> Nashville TN 37205

Who knows? If we all share enough stories, maybe we'll teach each other better ways to hit life's tough pitches.